Travel Adventures

EASTER ISLAND

Plotting Number Patterns

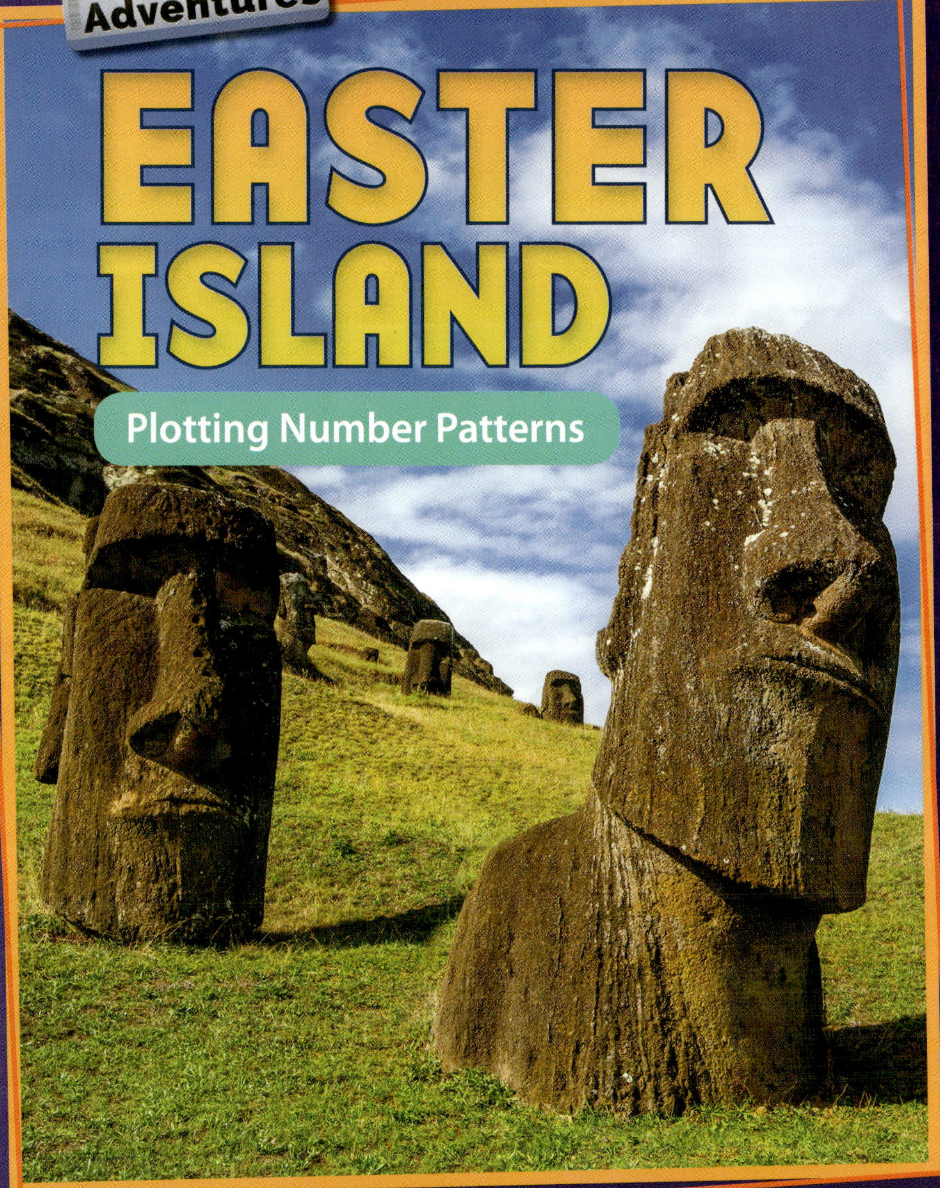

Kristy Stark, M.A.Ed.

Consultants

Lisa Ellick, M.A.
Math Specialist
Norfolk Public Schools

Pamela Estrada, M.S.Ed.
Teacher
Westminster School District

Publishing Credits

Rachelle Cracchiolo, M.S.Ed., *Publisher*
Conni Medina, M.A.Ed., *Managing Editor*
Dona Herweck Rice, *Series Developer*
Emily R. Smith, M.A.Ed., *Series Developer*
Diana Kenney, M.A.Ed., NBCT, *Content Director*
Stacy Monsman, M.A., *Editor*
Kristy Stark, M.A.Ed., *Editor*
Kevin Panter, *Graphic Designer*

Image Credits:
p.6 Yann Arthus-Bertrand/Getty Images; p.8 (top and bottom) DEA/W. Buss/Getty Images; p.9 (left) Cindy Hopkins/Alamy; p.9 (right) Rosanne Tackaberry/Alamy; p.10 Biosphoto/Alamy; p.15 Danita Delimont/Alamy; p.16 Dorling Kindersley/Getty Images; pp. 18–19 Mary Evans Picture Library/Alamy; p.20 Art Collection/Alamy; p.21 North Wind Picture Archives; p.22 Pictorial Press Ltd/Alamy; p.23 Classic Image/Alamy; p.25 (top) Robert Harding/Alamy; p.25 (bottom) Pulsar Imagens/Alamy; p.26 Globe Stock/Alamy; p.27 Marla Holden/Alamy; p.28 Universal Images Group North America LLC/Alamy; all other images from iStock and/or Shutterstock.

Library of Congress Cataloging-in-Publication Data

Names: Stark, Kristy, author.
Title: Travel adventures : Easter Island / Kristy Stark, M.A.Ed.
Other titles: Easter Island
Description: Huntington Beach, CA : Teacher Created Materials, 2018. | Audience: Grades 4 to 6. | Includes index.
Identifiers: LCCN 2017029064 (print) | LCCN 2017030917 (ebook) | ISBN 9781425859718 (eBook) | ISBN 9781425858254 (paperback)
Subjects: LCSH: Easter Island--Juvenile literature. | Easter Island--History--Juvenile literature. | Easter Island--Description and travel--Juvenile literature.
Classification: LCC F3169 (ebook) | LCC F3169 .S73 2018 (print) | DDC 919.61804--dc23
LC record available at https://lccn.loc.gov/2017029064

Teacher Created Materials
5301 Oceanus Drive
Huntington Beach, CA 92649-1030
http://www.tcmpub.com

ISBN 978-1-4258-5825-4

Made in China
Nordica.112017.CA21701237

Table of Contents

Welcome to Easter Island! 4

Birth of the Island 6

The First Inhabitants 9

Island Life and Culture 12

Explorers Arrive 20

Easter Island Today 24

Problem Solving 28

Glossary 30

Index 31

Answer Key 32

Welcome to Easter Island!

Easter Island is not a land of rabbits, colorful eggs, or spring flowers. It is a land with high peaks that were formed by volcanoes. It's a place with lakes of water in the **craters** of old volcanoes. Few trees dot its landscape. And, it is best known for more than 600 giant stone statues that give the island a sense of mystery.

Easter Island is a small island located in the Pacific Ocean. Like all islands, it is surrounded by water on all sides. Many people are not familiar with it. Only a small number of people live there. Few tourists visit. This is because Easter Island is so far from most places. Still, the **remote** island does get some visitors. The visitors exploring Easter Island see its lakes, craters, peaks, and famous statues.

Ecuador
Galápagos
Islands
(Ecuador)
Brazil
Peru
SOUTH
PACIFIC
OCEAN
Bolivia
Paraguay
Easter Island
Argentina
Chile

Birth of the Island

Islands are created by volcanic activity. It starts when **magma** rises from under Earth's crust. Magma eventually breaks through the ocean floor and becomes lava. When the lava cools, it leaves a formation of land.

This process formed the 63 square miles (163 square kilometers) of Easter Island. It is believed that the island was formed about half a million years ago. The volcanoes are now inactive. They no longer **spew** lava to add to the size of the island.

There are three main volcanoes that helped create the island. The island is shaped like a triangle. The three main volcanoes are found at each of the three points of the triangle.

The southwestern point is where Rano Kao (RAH-no cow) is found. It is the largest volcano on the island. It is so big that it can be seen from space!

Terevaka (TEHR-ih-vah-kah) is found on the northern point. It is the tallest volcano on the island. Its peak is about 1,969 feet (600 meters) above sea level.

The Poike (POY-kay) volcano is found on the east side of the island. It is the oldest of the three volcanoes.

LET'S EXPLORE MATH

Rano Kao is an inactive volcano. Rainwater accumulates in its crater. Imagine that scientists keep track of the total rainfall by recording the amount in a table each month.

Month	Total Rainfall (millimeters)
1	115
2	230
3	345
4	460
5	575

1. Describe the pattern.
2. If the pattern continues, what will the total rainfall be at the end of months 6, 10, and 12?

A team competes in a canoe competition.

The First Inhabitants

Easter Island is very remote. Because of this, no one knows for certain when the first people arrived on the island. It is estimated that the first people arrived around AD 400. The people only had stone tools on hand to build their boats. They sailed the boats from their home to the new island.

The first **inhabitants** called the island and themselves *Rapa Nui* (RAH-pah NOO-ee). The people who live there today still use this name.

It is likely that these people were **Polynesians**. But, the exact place they came from is not known. Some scientists think they came from the Marquesas (MAHR-kay-suhs) Islands. Other people think they came from Chile.

Wherever they came from, they traveled a long way to get there. The Marquesas Islands are more than 2,275 miles (3,662 kilometers) away. Chile is about 2,200 mi. (3,541 km) away.

The Rapa Nui people build their fishhooks and statues from bone and rock found on the island.

Why Did They Stay?

The reasons why people first came to Easter Island are debated. From any direction, an ocean crossing would have taken at least two weeks. The island did not have an **abundance** of resources. People still made the island their home. They found that the island provided all they would need to survive.

When people arrived, the island was covered with palm trees. Experts believe that people used palm trees for many things. Palm trees provided fruit to eat. They provided sap that could be used to make honey, syrup, and wine. Palm trees also provided necessary materials. Wood was used to construct homes. Wood was used to build canoes, too. Canoes allowed people to go into the ocean to hunt for animals, such as **porpoises**.

The island also has other plants and animals, such as toromiro (TOR-oh-meer-oh) trees, seals, parrots, and herons. People brought chickens, sweet potatoes, and bananas. These items, combined with the island's resources, helped them live and thrive.

toromiro trees

LET'S EXPLORE MATH

Toromiro trees used to grow in abundance on Easter Island. Now, they only grow in botanical gardens. Imagine that scientists plant a toromiro tree and record its height each year.

Year	Height (feet)
0	0
1	2
2	4
3	6
4	8
5	10
6	12
7	14
8	16

1. Write each year and height as an ordered pair.
2. Graph the ordered pairs on a coordinate plane.
3. How is the pattern shown in the table and graph?

Island Life and Culture

Early Rapa Nui people built the large statues for which Easter Island is known. These statues are called *moai* (MOH-eye). The first moai were made around AD 800. At first, they were small and round. They were only heads with eyes. Over time, the artists improved their skills. They could better shape the stones. So, they carved larger statues with more details. These moai had ears, noses, fingers, and other body parts. Experts think that the last moai were made as late as the 1860s.

The statues reflect the culture of the island's people. They built moai to honor their ancestors. They believed that their ancestors' spirits, or *mana*, continued to live after their deaths. So, statues were built to contain a person's spirit. They believed the spirits in the statues had influence over events in the physical world. Some moai have crowns made from a red stone. It is likely that the crowned moai were used in special **rituals**.

LET'S EXPLORE MATH

Imagine that two scientists spend a week studying moai. They each keep track of the total number of moai they examine.

Days	Scientist A's Total Number of Moai	Scientist B's Total Number of Moai
0	0	0
1	3	6
2	6	12
3	9	18
4	12	24
5	15	30
6	18	36
7	21	42

1. If the patterns continue, how many total moai will each scientist study after 30 days?
2. Other than Day 0, will there ever be a day when the scientists study the same total number of moai? How do you know?

Moai started as stones. The Rano Raraku (RAH-no RAH-rak-ew) volcano was the **quarry** that supplied these stones. The ash from this volcano was soft enough to carve. Some moai have red crowns. A crater called Puna Pau (Poo-nuh POW) was the source of the stone used to make the crowns.

People completed many steps to create moai. First, a large stone was chosen from the volcano. Next, an artist drew the moai onto the rock to determine its appearance. Then, the artist used tools to shape the rock into a statue.

When finished, moai did not stay at the quarry where they were made. Instead, they were moved to the village of the artist's ancestors. Some moai were moved as far as 14 mi. (23 km). This was not an easy task because many of the statues were enormous. The largest moai is about 32 ft. (10 m) tall and weighs about 82 tons (74,390 kilograms)!

After moving moai, people placed them so they faced the village. Moai were thought to watch over and protect everyone living there. So, people believed it was worth the work to move the tall, heavy moai.

LET'S EXPLORE MATH

Researchers conduct experiments to see how far they can move moai. Imagine that two research groups use a graph to record the total distance (in meters) they move moai during an experiment. Use the graph to answer the questions.

Distance Moai Are Moved

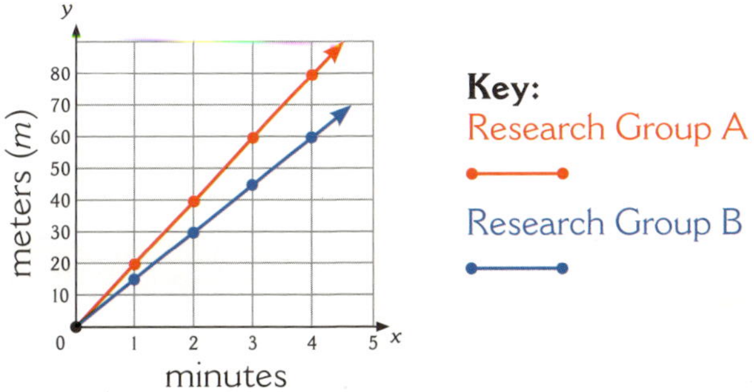

1. How far does each research group move the moai after 4 minutes?
2. If the patterns continue, how far will each group move the moai after 10 minutes?
3. Will the lines ever intersect? Why or why not?

Rano Raraku

Scientists are not sure how people moved the statues. They did not have the machines that exist today. They had to rely on stone, rope, wood, and human strength. Some experts think that people rolled the statues from the quarry. Others think that people used rope to tie statues to parts of tree trunks and pulled them to the villages. This method would have required hundreds of people. Regardless of how the moai were moved, it was an impressive **feat**.

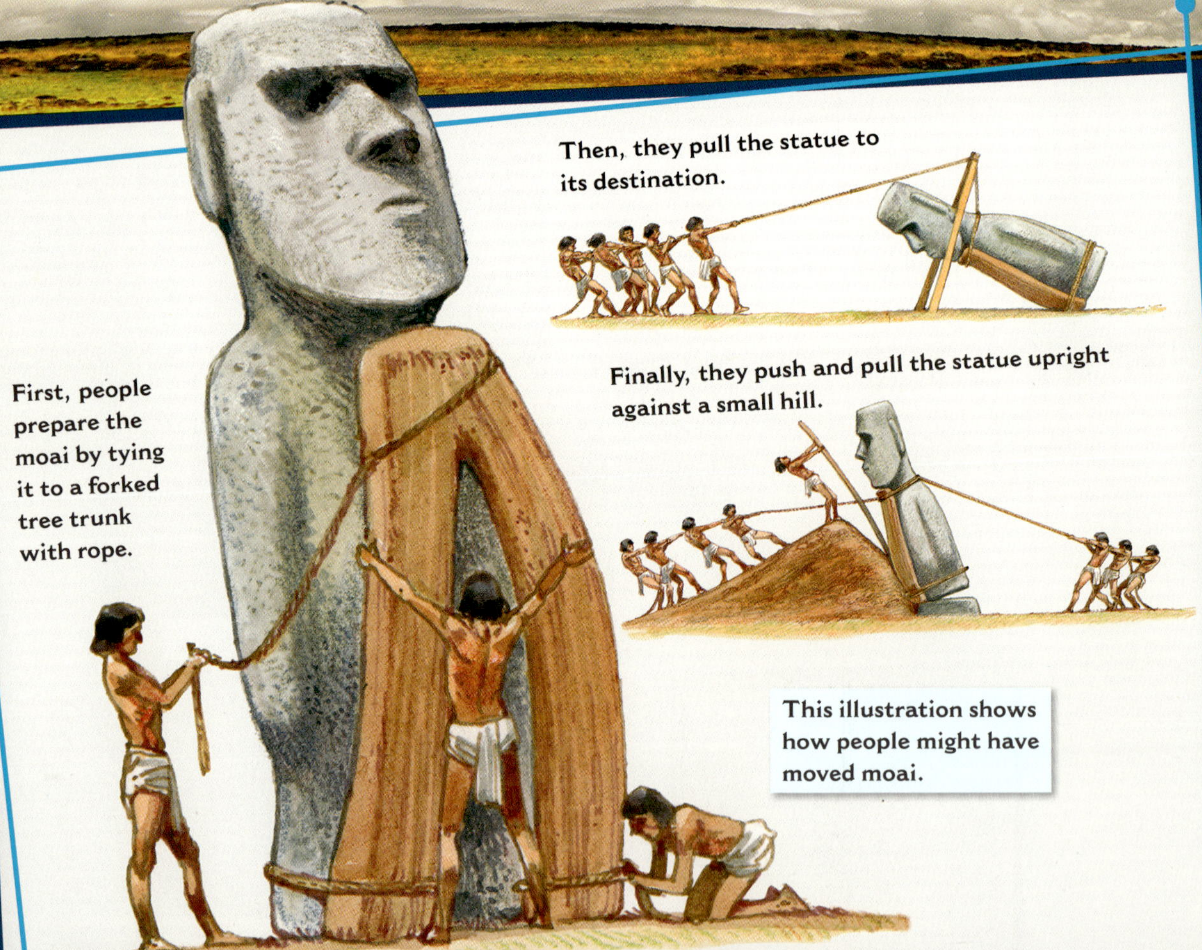

This illustration shows how people might have moved moai.

Conflict and Destruction

For several centuries, the people of Rapa Nui lived off the resources they had on the island. But, things changed during the 16th century. People used resources faster than they could **replenish** them. They used all the palm trees that were once abundant on the island. Soon, there weren't enough seeds to plant more trees. People could no longer rely on palm trees for food and wood. The island was very different from when people first arrived.

Without trees and other vegetation, the land itself began to **erode**. Topsoil used for growing crops washed away. Crops wouldn't grow. Consequently, less food was available.

Conflicts began as food and supplies became more **scarce**. People argued and fought over the few things that were left. The people of Rapa Nui split into several groups: the Short Ears, the Long Ears, and the Birdman Cult.

Wars broke out as people fought over resources. Experts think that the Birdman Cult knocked down the other groups' moai. The Birdman Cult may have also destroyed special shrines found near some moai called *ahus* (AH-hoos). Over 600 statues are left today. It makes people wonder how many moai were destroyed.

The culture and community of the island were destroyed, too. People became more violent. Many people were killed in battles for resources. Without trees for wood, people could not build boats to escape. There were few people left after the wars. Experts think there were as few as 750 survivors.

The people of Rapa Nui battle to the death.

LET'S EXPLORE MATH

Now, scientists plant trees on Easter Island to restart forests. Two types of trees they have planted are aito and eucalyptus. Imagine that the table shows the total number of each type of tree planted in a section of Easter Island over several years.

Year	Total Number of Aito Trees Planted	Total Number of Eucalyptus Trees Planted
0	0	0
1	160	40
2	320	80
3	480	120
4	640	160
5	800	200

1. Write each tree's data as a set of ordered pairs.
2. Graph both sets of ordered pairs on a coordinate plane.
3. Describe the patterns.

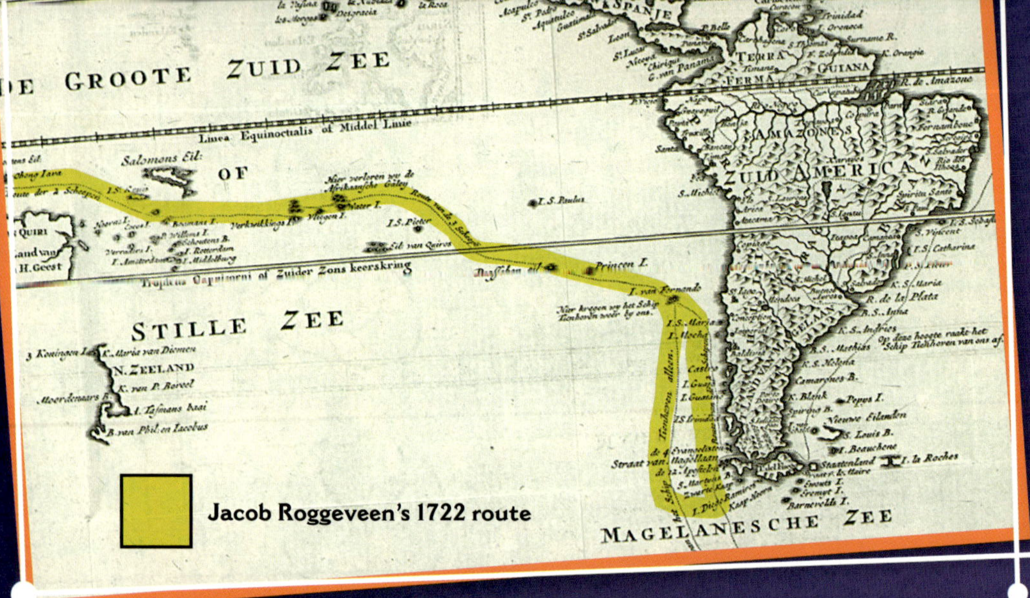

Explorers Arrive

A Dutch explorer named Jacob Roggeveen (RAHG-uh-veen) was the first European to arrive on the island in 1722. He found the island by mistake. He was looking for a place called *Terra Australis*. It was thought to be in the southern Pacific Ocean. He arrived on the island on Sunday, April 5. That day was the Easter holiday. He named the island *Paaseiland* (PAHS-ay-lauhnd), which means "Easter Island" in Dutch.

When he found the island, it had few trees. The trees there were less than 10 ft. (3 m) tall. He did not see any animals on the island. There were only about 2,000 people living there.

Roggeveen stayed on the island for only one day. There were strong winds that put his boats and crew in danger. Plus, the island did not have many resources. He and his crew left to continue their search for Terra Australis.

About 50 years later, more explorers arrived. In 1770, a Spanish explorer named Felipe González de Haedo (Feh-LEE-pay Gohn-ZAH-lehz de Ha-EH-doh) sailed from Peru to the island. His goal was to claim the island for Spain.

People visit Easter Island in the 1800s.

González de Haedo estimated that there were about 3,000 people on the island. The people did not fight against Spanish rule. Some chiefs signed a contract to let Spain claim the island. The chiefs were likely unable to read Spanish and didn't know the contract's meaning. The Spanish called the island San Carlos after their king, Carlos III. González de Haedo and his crew stayed on the island for less than a week. Then, they left. Spain did not send anyone back to the island to enforce Spanish rule.

Four years later, Sir James Cook arrived from Britain. In those four years, the island's population had decreased to about 700 men and fewer than 30 women. This was likely a result of the wars.

By 1877, there were only 111 people left on the island. Slave traders from Peru took people by force. Many of the remaining people died from diseases brought by the slave traders. The Rapa Nui people had never been exposed to smallpox.

In 1888, the island became part of Chile. In 1965, Chile appointed a governor to the island. The island's people became citizens of Chile.

Cook sails the HMS *Endeavour* to Easter Island.

Cook and his crew examine moai statues.

Easter Island Today

Today, there are about 6,000 people living on Rapa Nui. Most of them work to support the island's tourism. Tourists visit from all over the world. The island is far from other places, but tourists are willing to make the trip to see the island's history and culture.

In 1935, most of the island was made Rapa Nui National Park. The park was set up to keep the island's history and heritage safe. Lots of people want to see the moai. The statues are unlike any others on Earth. People visit the ahus, too. Fortunately, these historical remains are protected by rules that keep visitors from touching and destroying the history of the island.

People visit the volcanoes, too. They hike and bike to see them. They also take guided tours. They visit the lakes within the volcanic craters.

Visitors tour Rapa Nui National Park.

Tourists view the crater of Rano Kao.

Visitors can take part in the island's culture. It is alive and well! The Tapati (TUH-pah-tee) Festival takes place each year during the first two weeks of February. It was started in 1969 to **promote** and honor the island's culture. The **gala** includes many events. In sled races, men slide down the Maunga Pui (MAWN-guh Poo-ee) volcano on banana tree trunks. The festival has dancing, parades, and food, too. There is a swimming race in the sea. There is even a contest where people sing songs and tell legends about the island.

With all of the ways to see and experience the island's rich history and culture, tourism on Easter Island continues to rise. About 95,000 people visit each year. That number is up from about 30,000 people 10 years ago. As more people learn about Easter Island, tourism keeps growing. Perhaps you will visit the island some day. What would you like to see there?

A family sells souvenirs to tourists.

Musicians and dancers perform at the Tapati Festival.

LET'S EXPLORE MATH

One of the highlights of the Tapati Festival is a race in which competitors carry about 24 kilograms of bananas! Manu and Tane train for the triathlon by using patterns to increase the weight of the bananas they carry each week. The table below shows their training plans so far.

Week	Total Weight of Manu's Bananas (kg)	Total Weight of Tane's Bananas (kg)
0	0	0
1	3	6
2	6	12

If the patterns continue, how many weeks must each racer train to carry 24 kilograms of bananas?

Problem Solving

Luki (LOO-kee) and Tiare (TEE-are-ee) both live and work on Easter Island. They work as tour guides. From volcanoes to moai to the best surfing spots, they get paid to show people their island home.

Since Luki has 10 years of experience, he earns more for each tour than Tiare, who just started the job. Luki uses a table to track his earnings. Tiare uses a coordinate plane. Use their data on page 29 to compare their earnings.

1. Plot the data in Luki's table on a coordinate plane.
2. Use Tiare's coordinate plane to create a table of his earnings.
3. How many tours does each guide have to give to earn $90?
4. How much money does each guide earn after giving 12 tours? How do you know?

Number of Tours	Luki's Total Earnings ($)
0	0
1	45
2	90
3	135
4	180
5	225

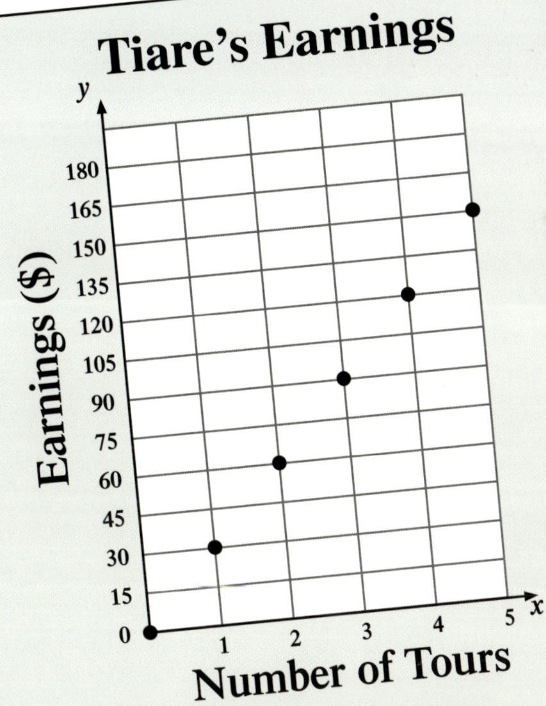

Glossary

abundance—a large amount of something

craters—bowl-shaped areas in the ground

erode—to move soil, mud, rock, and other particles away from an area

feat—an act that shows strength, skill, or courage

gala—a party or celebration

inhabitants—people who live in a certain place

magma—hot, melted rock

Polynesians—people from islands in the central and southern Pacific Ocean

porpoises—small whales with rounded noses

promote—to make people aware of something

quarry—a place where stones are dug from the ground

remote—far away

replenish—fill or build up again

rituals—series of acts that are always performed in the same way

scarce—uncommon

spew—to forcefully flow out